GROWING UP
to Praise God

THE MUFFIN FAMILY
GROWING UP WITH GOD SERIES®

V. GILBERT BEERS
Illustrated by HELEN ENDRES

HARVEST HOUSE PUBLISHERS
Eugene, Oregon 97402

GROWING UP TO PRAISE GOD

Copyright © 1987 by V. Gilbert Beers
Published by Harvest House Publishers
Eugene, Oregon 97402

Library of Congress Catalog Card
   Number 87-081045
ISBN 0-89081-527-5

All rights reserved. No portion of this book may be reproduced in any form without the written permission of the Publisher.

Printed in the United States of America.

BEFORE YOU READ

GROWING UP TO PRAISE GOD is designed to help your child praise God, not just on Sunday or when the Bible is read, but each day of the year, for each circumstance of life. Your child will learn to praise God when not-so-good things happen as well as the good.

This is a book of Bible stories and Muffin Family stories. The Muffin Family, a family much like the one you want your family to be, shows us how to live as God's friends should. Like the rest of us, they are not perfect, but they solve their problems the way God's friends should.

This book is part of the Muffin Family series, GROWING UP WITH GOD. Each story is really two stories—a Bible story, with a Bible truth about the way a Bible-time person praised God in daily life, and a Muffin Family story with that same Bible truth at work in a family much like yours.

Each story emphasizes one important Bible teaching. At the heart of that Bible teaching is a moral and spiritual value—*forgiveness, patience, kindness, love, thankfulness*, and others.

At the end of each Bible story/Muffin story couplet, you will find two pages of Muffin application, to help you and your child apply the Bible teaching and moral/spiritual value to the life of your child.

A color-coding system helps you find your way through this book. The book has four sections, "Praising God for What He Gives," "Praising God by What We Give," "Praising God by Saying No," and "Praising God by Singing." Each section has a different identifying color which begins on the contents page (What You Will Find in This Book) and continues throughout that section.

Bible stories have a color-coded line around the margin. Muffin Family stories have a color-coded bar at the bottom. Muffin application pages have a color-coded line around both pages. Each section title page has a large color-coded border. Labels at the bottom of the pages identify A Muffin Bible Story, A Muffin Family Story, and A Muffin Application.

The Muffin Family Growing Up With God series consists of:

Growing Up With Jesus
Growing Up With My Family
Growing Up to Praise God
Growing Up With God's Friends

TO PARENTS AND TEACHERS

When was the last time you praised God? What was it for? When was the last time your child praised God? Why?

One of the most important lessons we can teach our children is to praise God. We should praise Him in the morning, at noon, and at night. We should praise Him when things seem not-so-good as well as when things are going our way.

This book has Bible stories about people who praised God. With each one is a Muffin Family story about a family like yours who also praised God. Your child will learn to praise God, not because you explain how, but because he sees how these people did it.

Bible stories are retold in the language and thought of today. Bible people come alive so that your child feels at home with them. Bible truth also comes alive. What Mini Muffin learns is not much different from what Joseph learned.

Sometimes you will see a make-believe story, a touch of fantasy. We clearly mark these stories so your child will not confuse real life and fantasy. But fantasy is important in growing up.

So come with The Muffin Family into exciting adventures that will change your child's life. You'll be glad you did.

What You Will Find in This Book

PRAISING GOD FOR WHAT HE GIVES

- God's Wonderful Gift, Acts 3 — 8
  The Old Key, *A Muffin Make-believe Story* — 11
  Muffin Application — 14

- Someone Loves You, Matthew 27:35-44,55,56 — 16
  Ruff the Hero, *A Muffin Family Story* — 19
  Muffin Application — 22

PRAISING GOD BY WHAT WE GIVE

- A Boy's Small Gift, Matthew 14:13-21; Mark 6:30-44; Luke 9:10-17; John 6:1-15 — 26
  Two Small Gifts, *A Muffin Make-believe Story* — 29
  Muffin Application — 32

- Who Gave the Most? Mark 12:41-44; Luke 21:1-4 — 34
  Alphablock Gifts, *A Muffin Make-believe Story* — 37
  Muffin Application — 40

- Givers and Takers, Genesis 13:1-13 — 42
  GiGi's Giving Service, *A Muffin Make-believe Story* — 45
  Muffin Application — 48

PRAISING GOD BY SAYING NO

- Don't Touch That! Daniel 1 — 52
  "No!" *A Muffin Family Story* — 55
  Muffin Application — 58

- A Slave Who Said No, Genesis 39 — 60
  Does a Sissy Say No? *A Muffin Family Story* — 63
  Muffin Application — 66

- Don't Listen to Them! Matthew 27:15,16; Mark 15:6-15;
  Luke 23:13-25; John 18:39 —19:16 — 74
  Just Say No!, *A Muffin Make-believe Story* — 72
  Muffin Application — 76

PRAISING GOD BY SINGING

- Singing to a King, 1 Samuel 16:14-23 — 80
  Playing for Someone Special, *A Muffin Family Story* — 83
  Muffin Application — 86

- Praising God and Pleasing God, Nehemiah 8 — 88
  Sun Smiles and Cloud Tears, *A Muffin Make-believe Story* — 91
  Muffin Application — 94

PRAISING GOD
FOR WHAT HE GIVES

God's Wonderful Gift
Acts 3

"Please give me some money," the crippled man asked. Each day he sat at the large gate where people came into God's house, the Temple. Each day he begged for money.

That's what crippled or blind people had to do in Bible times. There were only enough jobs for strong healthy people. So what

could they do to get money? If they had no family they had to beg.

Sometimes people felt sorry for the man. They knew he had no other way to get money. So they gave him a small coin or two.

On this special day, Peter and John went to God's house to pray. As they went into God's house, the man cried out to them.

"May I have some money?" he asked.

Peter and John stopped. The man thought they would surely give him money now.

"Look at me!" Peter said to the man.

Slowly the beggar looked up at Peter. Then he held out his hand.

"I have no silver or gold coins to give you,"

Peter told the man. The man sadly looked away.

"But I have a much more wonderful gift for you," said Peter. "Jesus will heal your legs. Get up and walk."

Slowly the man stood on his feet. He took one step forward, then two. Then he jumped up and down.

"Praise God!" the man shouted. He had wanted one small coin. But God gave him a more wonderful gift than all the coins in the world. "Praise God!" the man kept saying. Isn't that what you would say too?

The Old Key

A Make-believe Story Poppi told to Mini and Maxi

A man sat by the side of the road, begging for money. He was too old to work, and he had no one to take care of him. There was no other way for him to get money.

Some people laughed at the old man. Others passed by without looking at him. But a few stopped and gave him a coin or two.

No one gave him very much. So the old man was always hungry. He never had enough to eat.

One special day the old man saw a prince coming down the road. He was sure the prince would laugh at him or not even look at him. But the prince stopped and talked with the old man.

"You look hungry," said the prince.

"I am," said the old man. "If you could give me one small coin it would help."

The prince smiled. "I will give you something much more wonderful than that," he said. "If you use it wisely, something good will happen to you."

Then the prince gave the man an old key. It didn't look like it was worth much.

The prince smiled and walked away. The old man looked at the key again. He was hungry. He could not eat an old key. So he almost threw it away. But then he began to think.

"The prince is a wise man," he thought. "I will follow him. Perhaps I will learn to use his key wisely."

So the old man hobbled along far behind the prince. That was certainly a wise thing to do, wasn't it?

At last the prince went through a large wooden door. When he was inside, the door closed tight.

The old man sat down beside the door. What should he do now? He sat by the door for a long time to think.

At last he looked at the key again. Then he saw these words written on it, "By Me if any man enter in, he shall be saved."

"I have read those words before," the old man thought.

Then he looked again at the door. Above it these words were written, "I am the Door."

Suddenly the old man saw a keyhole in the door. It was exactly the shape of his key.

The old man trembled as he put the key in the door and turned it. When he opened the door he could hardly believe his eyes. There was the prince, standing beside a beautiful table filled with wonderful food.

"Come and eat with me at my table," said the prince. "You may come whenever you wish. The old key will always let you in. You will always have plenty of good food here with me."

What do you think the old man did then? What would you have done?

Growing Is...
Expecting Good Gifts from God

What the Bible Story Teaches
God has better gifts for us than we expect. When we ask God for something good, let's not be surprised if He gives us something wonderful.

Thinking about the Bible Story
1. What gift did the crippled man want? What gift did God give him instead?
2. Why was the gift God gave much better than the gift he wanted?

What the Muffin Story Teaches
God has many wonderful things for us. We must thank Him when He gives them to us.

Thinking about the Muffin Story
1. How does this story remind you of the Bible story? Read Psalm 23:5. How does this story remind you of this verse?
2. Read John 10:9. Who is The Door? Do you think Jesus wants to give you good things? Do you thank Him when He does?

What Are Some Good Gifts That God Gives?

1. The sun to keep me warm.
2. Rain to make things grow.
3. Green grass for my lawn.
4. Birds to sing to me.
5. Trees to give me fruit.
6. A brother or sister to play with me.

The Bible Says
God can do much more for us than we ask or think (from Ephesians 3:20).

Prayer
Dear Jesus, thank You for giving me so many good gifts. Show me how to use them for You. Amen.

Someone Loves You
Matthew 27:35-44,55,56

"Don't hurt Him," Jesus' friends whispered.

"Crucify Him," the Pharisees and their friends shouted.

"Nail Him to the cross," the Roman soldiers ordered.

But Jesus said nothing. He was quiet even when the soldiers nailed His hands and feet to the cross.

Jesus began to pray. "Father, forgive them," He said.

The Roman soldiers were ashamed when they heard that. "We nail Him to the cross and He prays for us," they said. They could

see that Jesus was not like anyone else.

The soldiers picked up a sign. It said, "Jesus of Nazareth, King of the Jews." They nailed it on His cross.

"Is He a king?" one of them asked.

"He acts better than a king," another answered.

When Jesus' cross was set up, people came to watch Him die. The Pharisees mocked him. The soldiers gambled for His robe. Jesus' friends cried.

The sky grew dark over the hill where Jesus was crucified. By noon it looked like evening. Some people were afraid, so they ran away.

In the middle of the afternoon, Jesus cried out, "It is finished! Father, I give My spirit into Your hands." Then Jesus died.

The man in charge of the soldiers looked

at Jesus. "He is God's Son," he said softly.

It's sad to think of Jesus dying, isn't it? But that's why He came to earth. He loved you and me so much that He came to die for us. That was Jesus' way of saying, "I love you very much. I want you to live in My home with Me forever."

When you love someone very much, you will do anything for that person, won't you? You will remember to thank Jesus for what He did, won't you? You will love Him for doing what He did for you and me.

Ruff the Hero

Maxi sat up in bed and listened. He was sure that he had heard a strange noise downstairs.

"What should I do?" Maxi wondered. "Should I go downstairs to see what it is? Or should I wake Poppi?"

Maxi decided that he didn't want to wake Poppi just to tell him he thought he heard a noise. That seemed foolish. He would go down quietly and check things himself.

Maxi slipped from his bed and tiptoed down

the carpeted stairway, with Ruff behind him. Maxi went so quietly that he could hardly hear himself breathe.

But as soon as Maxi went into the living room, he said "OH" before he could catch himself. There on the other side of the room was the dark shadowy form of a burglar.

The burglar heard Maxi and swung around. When he saw that Maxi was a boy, he ran for him.

"Snoopy kid," he growled. "I'll get you!"

When Ruff saw the burglar rush at Maxi he exploded like a stick of dynamite (or dogamite as Maxi said later), leaping at the burglar with a bundle of growls, barks, woofs and every other noise he could make.

Ruff's noises brought Poppi into the room. By this time the burglar decided that he had better find another home to rob. He flung Ruff against the wall as hard as he could and ran out.

Mommi and Mini rushed in, just in time to see Maxi bend over poor Ruff, who was lying on the floor. "Did someone kill our Ruff?" Mini asked.

Maxi put his ear against Ruff's chest to listen for his heartbeat. "He's alive," said Maxi. "I can hear his heart beating."

Mommi put a cold cloth on the bump on Ruff's head. Then all the Muffin family sat with Ruff and prayed for him.

"That burglar could have killed you," Poppi told Maxi. "But Ruff saved you. He was willing to die for you."

Maxi looked down at Ruff. "Oh, Ruff, thank you for doing that for me," said Maxi. "I love you even more because you were willing to die for me."

"That's why we love Jesus so much, isn't it?" Mini added.

After a long time Ruff began to move. Then he stood on his feet and licked Maxi's face. "Thank you, my special friend," Maxi said to Ruff. "Thank you for saving my life. And thank you for helping me understand more what Jesus did for me."

A MUFFIN FAMILY STORY • 21

Growing Is . . . Giving to Those We Love

What the Bible Story Teaches
Jesus died for us because He loved us so much.

Thinking about the Bible Story
1. How do you know that Jesus loves you? What special thing did He do for you?
2. Are you glad that Jesus loves you? Why?

What the Muffin Story Teaches
When you love someone you will do good things for that person.

Thinking about the Muffin Story
1. Why was Ruff willing to die for Maxi? Would he have done that if he had not loved Maxi? Why not?
2. If you were Maxi, would you love Ruff even more for what he did? Why?
3. How did Ruff help Maxi understand better what Jesus did for him?

How Can I Show Jesus I Love Him?

Which of these would show Jesus that you love Him?

1. Talk with Him each day.
2. Read my Bible each day.
3. Argue with my brother or sister.
4. Tell a friend about Jesus.
5. Learn about Jesus at God's house.

The Bible Says
God loves you so much that He sent His only son to die for you (from John 3:16).

Prayer
Thank You, Jesus, for dying for me. I know You love me very much. Now I want to show my love for You. Amen.

A MUFFIN APPLICATION • 23

PRAISING GOD
BY WHAT WE GIVE

A Boy's Small Gift

Matthew 14:13-21; Mark 6:30-44; Luke 9:10-17; John 6:1-15

"Please may I go?" a boy begged his mother.

"Go where?" his mother asked.

"All my friends are going to listen to Jesus," he said. "May I go too?"

The mother smiled. "Of course," she said. "I wish I could go too, but I can't. Hurry and wash while I get something for you to eat."

The boy grumbled about washing. But by the time he finished, his mother had put two dried fish and five little loaves of bread like buns into a basket.

The boy was excited as he ran across the hills to find Jesus. At last he saw a big crowd of people. They were sitting on the hillside, listening to Jesus.

The boy walked up to the front, where Jesus was teaching. Then he put his basket on the grass and sat beside it.

The boy listened quietly. Everyone else listened quietly too. They listened to everything Jesus said.

Toward evening some of Jesus' friends came to see Him. The boy could hear what they said.

"There is no food here in this lonely place," they told Jesus. "Should we send the people away to get food?"

"No, you give them something to eat," Jesus said.

Jesus' friends looked surprised. "But where will we get enough food for all these people?" they asked. "Should we buy it?"

"How much food do we have here now?" Jesus asked.

Jesus' friends walked through the crowd. When they came back they said, "No one has any food except this boy."

The boy had almost forgotten about the food his mother had given him. "Here, you may have it," he said. "It isn't much, but I want Jesus to have it."

Jesus smiled and thanked the boy. "Ask the people to sit in groups of fifty or a hundred," He told His friends.

Jesus began to break the bread and fish. His friends took the pieces to the people. Jesus kept on breaking the bread and fish and people kept on eating. At last all the people had eaten as much as they wanted.

The boy could hardly believe it! His small gift to Jesus had fed five thousand people. Think what Jesus can do with your small gifts too!

Two Small Gifts

A Make-believe Story Mommi Told Maxi and Mini about a Visit to Muffkinland

Once there were two Muffkins who lived in Muffkinland. Givvy Muffkin was wise and loyal to his king. Greedy Muffkin was selfish and not so loyal. But both were hungry because there was no food at this time.

One day the two Muffkins set out to seek their fortune, which would be something to eat. They looked near and far until at last they found a treasure—ten grains of corn.

Greedy Muffkin rubbed his hands. "We will divide the treasure equally," he said. "Four for you and six for me!"

Givvy Muffkin watched Greedy scoop up six grains, pop them into a big sack, and head home. Then Givvy placed his four grains into a sack and whistled as he headed home.

Greedy rushed into his Muffkin house, closed the door and hid his six grains. He would feast on them alone for many days.

Givvy thought once about doing the same. But on his way home he thought of the king and wanted to share his treasure with him.

"I want to share these equally with you," Givvy told the king. "Two for you and two for me."

Two grains did not seem like much for a king, but they were half of Givvy's treasure.

"I thank you with all my heart," said the king. "Your two grains will become a royal feast for all the kingdom."

"But how?" asked Givvy.

"By five miracles," said the king.

The king tucked the two grains of corn under the warm soil in the palace garden.

"The miracle of the soil is God's first miracle," said the king.

Then a big cloud moved across the sun and dropped its rain upon the soil. "The miracle of the rain is God's second miracle," said the king.

When the cloud left the sun smiled. The moist soil was like a cozy blanket over the grains of corn. "The miracle of the sun is God's third miracle," said the king.

Before long green shoots came from the soil. They became big stalks of corn. "The miracle of new life is God's fourth miracle," said the king.

By autumn the stalks turned golden brown. Then the king ordered his men to climb the stalks and cut the golden ears from them. "God's fifth miracle is multiplication," said the king. "From your two seeds have come a feast for the kingdom."

And what a royal feast it was. Of course, Givvy was the guest of honor. His two small gifts had become a feast for the kingdom.

Growing Is . . .
Giving, Even Small Gifts

What the Bible Story Teaches
Jesus can do wonderful things with even our smallest gifts.

Thinking about The Bible Story
1. How many people did Jesus feed with the boy's small gift?
2. How could Jesus feed so many people with so little food?
3. Did Jesus need a bigger gift? Why not?

What the Muffin Story Teaches
Even our smallest gifts can do much good to others.

Thinking about the Muffin Story
1. How did Greedy Muffkin divide the grains of corn? How did Givvy divide them with the king? What does this tell you about each of them?
2. What were the five miracles? How does each miracle help food grow?
3. Why should you be willing to give even small gifts for Jesus' work?

The Bible Says
Give and God will give even more back to you (from Luke 6:38).

Prayer
Dear Jesus, thank You for Your wonderful gifts. Please accept my small gifts for You. Amen.

Who Gave the Most?
Mark 12:41-44; Luke 21:1-4

Jesus and His friends often went to God's house together. Sometimes they prayed. Sometimes Jesus taught them about God. Sometimes they just talked with each other.

One day when Jesus and His friends came to God's house, which was called the Temple, they went into a large courtyard with a stone floor. Everyone met there to talk. Some bought birds and animals from men who had set up little booths.

Money changers shouted to people who

passed by. People could not spend foreign money in God's house. They had to trade it for the kind of money that could be spent there. Of course, the money changers charged extra to do that. Most of the time they charged too much.

From there Jesus and His friends walked into the next courtyard. It was quiet in this place. No birds or animals were sold. No one shouted or traded money. This was the place people gave money.

Along the wall were strange looking boxes.

Each had an opening that looked like a curved horn. People put their money in the top of the horn. People used that money to take care of God's house.

Jesus sat by the wall, across from the boxes. He watched as people came and dropped in their offering.

One man dropped gold coins into a box. It was a lot of money. Another man dropped in even more gold coins. A third man gave even more than the other two.

At last a poor widow came in. She dropped in two small copper coins. They were called mites. They were not worth much.

"Who gave the most money?" Jesus asked.

Jesus' friends were surprised. Of course the rich men gave the most.

"The poor widow gave the most," Jesus said. "The rich men gave extra money they did not need. But this poor woman gave all the money she had."

Jesus' friends looked at each other. He was right. Anyone can give extra money. But it takes a special person to give everything.

Alphablock Gifts

A Make-believe Story Poppi Told Maxi about His Toys in Toyland

Have you ever seen an alphablock tower? Perhaps you have made one. It's a tower made of blocks with letters on them.

One day Maxi's toys in Toyland decided they would make an alphablock tower. It would be the tallest one ever built in Toyland.

"Bring your alphabet blocks to the Toyland gate," a wooden soldier announced. "Bring all you can. We must make this the tallest tower ever."

Before long a wooden soldier came with an alphabet block on his shoulder. Another wooden soldier pulled some blocks in a little red wagon. And another pushed some blocks in a little wheelbarrow.

One by one the blocks were made into a tower. Before long, a wooden soldier had to get a ladder to put on the next block.

"We need more alphabet blocks," said the soldier on the ladder. But by this time the

wooden soldiers had given half their blocks. Jack-in-the-Box and Nutcracker had given half of theirs too. So had the china doll. They had all given all they WANTED to give.

Suddenly trumpets tooted and wooden soldiers stood at attention. "Here comes the king," some toys shouted.

"And look at his wagon loaded with blocks," said a soldier. "That's all we need and more."

Everyone watched as the king pulled up to the tower. He gave the command and the soldiers began to unload blocks.

"One, two, three," counted one soldier.

"Four, five," counted another.

Then they stopped counting. That's because the king commanded the soldiers to stop taking blocks.

"Only FIVE blocks?" asked some soldiers. "He could have given ten blocks and still have half of his blocks left."

But that was all the king WANTED to give. So the tower was not finished.

"We need three more blocks," said the wooden soldier at the top of the ladder.

"But where will we get them?" asked another. "Everyone has given all he wants to give."

"Look!" said a wooden soldier. He pointed down the street.

Here came the Windup Mouse, pushing a little wheelbarrow. It had three blocks on it.

One by one the blocks were unloaded. One by one they were carried up the ladder. One by one they were put on the tower.

"Three?" a soldier asked. "That's all Windup Mouse has. He gave everything!"

"Hooray, hooray," the wooden soldiers shouted. "We've build the tallest alphablock tower ever."

"Hooray, hooray for Windup Mouse," said the Jack-in-the-Box. "He gave the most. He gave all he had."

Do you think Jack-in-the-Box was right?

A MUFFIN FAMILY STORY • 39

Growing Is . . . Wanting to Give

What the Bible Story Teaches
Giving a little because you want to give is better than giving a lot because you have to give.

Thinking about the Bible Story
1. Who gave more coins, the widow or the rich men? Who kept more?
2. Why did Jesus say the widow gave more than these men?
3. What would you like to say to this widow now?

What the Muffin Story Teaches
How much you give is not as important as how you want to give.

Thinking about the Muffin Story

1. Who gave the most blocks?
2. Who kept the most blocks?
3. Why did Jack-in-the-Box say Windup Mouse gave the most? Was he right? Why?

Does Maxi Want to Give?

Mommi and Poppi asked Maxi to give Mini a birthday gift. Which of these says he wants to give it?

1. Aw, do I have to?
2. I'll be glad to.
3. Why?
4. She didn't give me one.
5. That will be fun.

The Bible Says
God is glad when we give because we want to give (from 2 Corinthians 9:7).

Prayer
Dear Jesus, You gave Yourself for me because You wanted to do it. That's why I give to You too. Amen.

Givers and Takers
Genesis 13:1-13

Abraham was a giver. Lot was a taker. Takers like to get all they can from givers. That's the way Lot was with his Uncle Abraham.

When Lot was a little boy his father Haran died. There was no one else to help Lot, so Uncle Abraham took care of him. He treated Lot like his own son.

Abraham worked hard and became rich. He helped Lot become rich too. Abraham had flocks and herds. He had sheep, oxen, donkeys, and camels. But he also helped Lot build up flocks and herds too.

Lot should have been happy. He should have loved his generous uncle. He should have wanted his uncle to have the best. Instead, Lot wanted more. He wanted the best. That's the way takers are.

Before long the people who took care of Lot's animals began to quarrel with the people who took care of Abraham's animals. Then they began to fight.

"What will the neighbors think?" Abraham

asked sadly. The neighbors were the people of Canaan. They did not believe in Abraham's God. They worshiped idols instead.

"We're family," Abraham told Lot. "We must not fight. Choose the part of the land you want. I will take what is left."

In Abraham's time that was the polite thing to say. If Lot had been polite he would have let his Uncle Abraham have the best.

But Lot was not polite. He was a taker.

"I want that!" Lot said. He chose the best for himself.

"Then I will take what is left," Abraham said sadly. So Lot the taker moved to his rich land. Abraham the giver sadly watched him go.

GiGi's Giving Service

A Make-believe Story Mommi Told Mini about Her Stuffed Animal Friends on Thimblelane Trails

One day Maxi and Mini were visiting Buffy Bear at his home on Thimblelane Trails.

"This is exciting, Buffy Bear," said Mini. "I always thought you and Todie and GiGi and the others were just stuffed animals. But today you're like real people."

"It's exciting for us too!" said Buffy Bear. "We thought you were just squishy people. Now you're like real stuffed animals."

"Speaking of stuffed things," said Maxi. "Isn't that Grabbie up there in a booth?"

"It is!" said Mini. "But Grabbie, what are you doing in that strange booth?"

"Look at the sign," said Grabbie. "I've set up business—Grabbie's Grabbing Service."

"But what are you grabbing?" asked Mini.

"Whatever I can get from the booth next door," said Grabbie.

Maxi and Mini had not noticed the booth next door. Then they saw it. And they saw Mini's calico goose GiGi in the booth.

"GiGi!" said Mini. "But what is GiGi's Giving Service?"

"Just what it says," GiGi said with a smile. "I specialize in giving to needy stuffed animals along Thimblelane Trails."

Just then Grabbie appeared, wearing a

ragged top hat. "Pardon me, dear lady," he said. "I'm collecting for the poor who lost their homes in a big flood."

"Oh, dear," said GiGi. "I didn't hear about the flood. But I do have one golden egg I laid yesterday." Grabbie ran away as soon as GiGi gave him the golden egg.

"That was Grabbie," Mini whispered to Maxi. "He's being a taker and GiGi is being a giver. I don't like the way he's doing it."

Just then Grabbie knocked on GiGi's booth door again. This time he had on an old fireman's hat.

"Pardon me, dear lady," he said. "I'm collecting for firemen who got burned in a fire."

"Oh, dear," said GiGi. "I didn't hear about the fire. But I do have one golden egg I laid last night." Grabbie grabbed the golden egg and ran away.

Grabbie had hardly left before he came back with a cook's hat on. This time he asked for help for the poor who lost their kitchen stoves in a big wind.

"I just love to give to these needy causes," said GiGi. This time she had to lay a golden egg.

"Stop!" said Mini. "Are you really having fun Grabbie?" she asked.

Grabbie looked sad. "No, I'm really not," he said. "I think GiGi is having much more fun than I am."

"Then let's put these two businesses together," said Mini. Grabbie and GiGi thought that was a wonderful idea and named it "Grabbie's 'n' GiGi's Giving Service." Do you like it?

Growing Is . . .
Giving More than Getting

What the Bible Story Teaches
There are givers and takers. Takers are sad to watch. Givers bring us joy.

Thinking about the Bible Story
1. Was Lot a giver or taker? How do you know?
2. Was Abraham a giver or taker? How do you know?
3. Which man makes you happier? Why?

What the Muffin Story Teaches
Giving is more fun than getting.

Thinking about the Muffin Story

1. Was GiGi having fun giving? How do you know?
2. Was Grabbie having fun grabbing? How do you know?
3. Why do you think Grabbie will have more fun in the giving business?

Which Friend Is Having More Fun?

Which of Maxi's and Mini's friends is having more fun? Why?

1. Pookie says, "I want the biggest piece of birthday cake!"
2. Charlie says, "Make me pitcher or I'll take my ball and go home."
3. BoBo says, "We'll share."
4. Big Bluffo says, "We're going to play this game my way or not at all."
5. Maria says, "Let me help you."

The Bible Says
It is better to give than to get (from Acts 20:35).

Prayer
Dear Jesus, teach me how much fun it is to give. Amen.

PRAISING GOD BY SAYING NO

Don't Touch That!
Daniel 1

"You four young men have an important job here in Babylon," an officer said. Daniel and his three friends did not want an important job in Babylon. They wanted to be home in Israel. But they knew they could not go home. The soldiers of Babylon had captured them. They had burned the beautiful city of Jerusalem and brought Daniel and his friends here to Babylon.

"You will go to our best schools and learn to be officers. You will be treated well," the officer told them. "Some day you may even work for the king."

The four young men must have worried a little when their names were changed to Babylonian names. They would no longer be called by their Hebrew names.

They worried even more when they learned what they would eat. It was the same food and wine given to the king. Should they eat it? Some of it was pig meat. God's law had told them not to eat that. Most of the food had been offered to idols. God's people should certainly not eat that! And they did not want to drink the king's wine either.

Should they eat the food and not fuss about it? Or should they do what they thought God wanted them to do and say no.

Daniel made up his mind. He would say no. The others decided to be like Daniel.

Daniel talked with the officer, who was named Ashpenaz. As nicely as he could, he asked Ashpenaz to give them other good food instead.

Ashpenaz liked Daniel. He wanted to help. But he was worried. "What if your food makes you thinner than the other men?" he asked. "The king will cut off my head."

"May we try it for ten days?" Daniel asked.

That seemed fair enough. So Ashpenaz gave Daniel and his friends other food for ten days. They had said no, but in a nice way.

Daniel and his friends did not get thinner. They were even healthier than the other men. Ashpenaz was happy.

Daniel and his friends were happy. They had pleased God by saying no. Now they knew that God was with them. He would take care of them, for they had been faithful to Him.

"No!"

When Maxi went to school Monday morning he was still thinking about the Sunday school lesson. They had talked about Daniel and his friends. They had talked about the way Daniel said "no" and would not eat the king's food or drink his wine.

"So what does that have to do with us?" Pookie had asked in Sunday school. "No king is going to offer his food and wine to us kids. And what hamburgers have been offered to idols?"

Pookie's friends had thought that was a good point. So Maxi was still thinking about it on the way to school. Maybe Pookie was right. No king would offer him food or wine today. He certainly didn't expect to get a hamburger offered to an idol.

"So what?" Maxi almost said aloud.

A MUFFIN FAMILY STORY • 55

When classes began Maxi was too busy to think about Daniel and the king's food. And when lunchtime came he was too busy thinking about his own food. So by the time school was over Maxi had forgotten about Daniel.

Maxi came out of school and headed down the sidewalk toward home. Then he heard someone whisper his name.

"Psssst! Maxi!"

Maxi looked. There were three of his school friends. They were standing by some bushes.

"Come here!" they whispered. "We've got something to show you."

Maxi walked over to the bushes. One of the boys pulled a bright package from his pocket.

"Look what I've got!" he said. "We're going behind the bushes with this stuff. Come on."

Maxi's heart began to pound. He had never done that before. Something inside said, "Go on! Maybe it's fun!"

Suddenly Maxi seemed to see Mommi's and Poppi's and Mini's smiling faces. He knew they would not want him to do this.

"Sorry fellows," said Maxi. He turned to leave.

"Sissy!" one of them hissed. Maxi bristled.

"Are you a boy or a man?" another whispered.

Maxi took a step back toward his friends. His heart began to pound again. Maybe just once wouldn't hurt.

Suddenly Maxi seemed to see the picture of Jesus on his bedroom wall. Jesus would not want him to do this. Then he remembered Daniel. Daniel said no. So would he.

"He's tied to his mommi's apron strings," another boy said.

Maxi didn't care what the boys said. He wanted to please Jesus. He wanted to be like Daniel.

"Sorry fellows!" he said. "Jesus doesn't want me to do that with you. And I want to please Jesus more than you." Maxi thought that was the best "no" he could say.

Maxi whistled as he walked home. Now he thought he saw his picture of Jesus again. This time Jesus was smiling.

Growing Is . . . Learning to Say No

What the Bible Story Teaches
Does God want you to do something? Do it! Does He want you not to do something? Say no!

Thinking about the Bible Story
1. What did Ashpenaz want Daniel to do?
2. Why did Daniel say no?
3. Would you have said no? Why?

What the Muffin Story Teaches
Jesus is pleased when we say no to things we shouldn't do.

Thinking about the Muffin Story
1. What did Maxi's friends say to him?
2. Who would not want Maxi to do this?
3. Why did Maxi say no? Why do you think this pleased Jesus?

Will You Say No?

Will you say no if a friend asks you to:

1. Say something bad about a friend?
2. Steal an apple?
3. Lie to your mother?
4. Tell him about Jesus?
5. Throw junk on a neighbor's lawn?
6. Go behind some bushes to smoke or drink with "the gang."

The Bible Says
Don't touch unclean things, don't do things that are not right (from 2 Corinthians 6:17).

Prayer
Dear Jesus, I want to please You by what I do. I also want to please You by what I don't do. Amen.

A Slave Who Said No
Genesis 39

Joseph was a slave in Egypt. That's because his brothers became angry and sold him.

"God is with me," Joseph kept saying to himself. "He will take care of me."

Joseph watched the Egyptians who came to buy. Which one would be his new master?

Joseph must have prayed many times for God to help him. Suddenly a man with a kind face came toward Joseph. He watched as Joseph stood tall and fearless. He knew that Joseph was no ordinary slave.

"I will buy him," the kind man said to the traders. "He will make a fine servant in my household."

Joseph worked hard for Potiphar, the kind man. Whatever Potiphar asked, Joseph did quickly. He even did many good things that Potiphar did not expect him to do.

Potiphar noticed how things changed since Joseph came. He saw that Joseph prayed to

God and tried to please Him. Soon Potiphar knew that God was with Joseph.

One day Potiphar had a talk with Joseph. "Things have gone well since you came," he said. "So I am putting you in charge of all the things in my house."

God kept on doing good things to Potiphar's household because of Joseph. Soon Potiphar put Joseph in charge of everything that he owned.

But Potiphar's wife fell in love with Joseph. One day she saw Joseph alone.

"Come here and pretend that I am your wife," she said.

"No. I can't do that," Joseph told her. "Potiphar has done so much for me. How could I do this to him?"

Each day Potiphar's wife kept trying. One day when they were alone, she grabbed Joseph's cloak. Joseph ran from the room.

When Potiphar came home, his wife told lies about Joseph. She said Joseph had tried to hurt her.

Potiphar was angry. He had Joseph thrown into prison.

"Why did this happen? Will God be with me here?" Joseph must have wondered each day. Joseph did not know it then, but there in that prison he would meet someone who would take him to Pharaoh. When that happened, Pharaoh would make him ruler of all Egypt. God was helping Joseph become ruler of Egypt. But Joseph had to go to prison first. God does know what He is doing, doesn't He?

Does a Sissy Say No?

Maxi invited Pookie and Big Bluffo to a tree house party. Mini invited her friends to a tea party. The problem was that Mini's tea party was under Maxi's tree house where he was having his tree house party.

Mini and her friends were not really drinking tea, only pretend tea. Maxi and his friends were not really having a party, only a talk-time.

When Mini and her friends said something funny all of them giggled. When girls giggle, boys in tree houses above them get ideas.

"I can't believe those giggly girls would have their tea party down there," Big Bluffo said.

"Why not?" Maxi asked.

"Well, I can think of several good reasons," said Big Bluffo. "Like water balloons, pepper that floats from tree houses, or a sky full of pink drink that rains down."

"You wouldn't dare do that!" said Maxi.

"Oh yes I would," said Big Bluffo. "And Pookie will help me, WON'T YOU POOKIE?"

Pookie was always chicken around Big Bluffo. He was afraid of him. So he gulped and nodded his head yes.

"Well you can't do that to my little sister," said Maxi. "And that's that!"

Big Bluffo slapped his leg and laughed. "Pookie, did you hear what I heard?" he sneered. "This kid is actually trying to protect his sister. You could wrap my sister in cookie dough and bake her in the oven and I wouldn't care. We're always fighting."

A MUFFIN FAMILY STORY • 63

"Well, Mini and I aren't always fighting, just sometimes," said Maxi. "Anyway, leave her alone or go home."

Maxi sounded so tough that Big Bluffo knew he meant it.

"OK, SISSY, I will go home," he said. Then Big Bluffo began to climb down the ladder. On the way he gave Mini's table a big bump and spilled her pretend tea over the table.

"That's for having a SISSY for a brother," Big Bluffo growled at Mini.

That night at the dinner table Mini could see that Maxi was sad. "Why did Big Bluffo call you a sissy?" she asked.

Poppi and Mommi thought Mini was trying to start an argument. Poppi coughed a little fake cough and Mommi looked over her glasses at Mini.

"Oh, Big Bluffo didn't like something I said," Maxi answered.

"Like what?" Mini asked.

Poppi coughed again and looked sternly at Mini. Mommi looked over her glasses again. "Really, Mini!" she said.

"That's OK," said Maxi. "I just told him to go home."

"But why?" Mini prodded.

"MINI!" said Mommi. "REALLY!"

"Because he wanted to drop water balloons on your tea party," said Maxi. "I told him to go home and he called me a sissy."

"Thanks, Maxi!" said Mini. "But I'm sorry you had an argument with Big Bluffo because of me."

"I think Joseph settled Maxi's argument a long time ago," said Poppi.

"Who?" Maxi asked.

"Joseph, in the Bible. Joseph was faithful to God and Potiphar, the man he worked for," said Poppi. "When Potiphar's wife wanted Joseph to do something wrong, Joseph said no. He knew that would hurt Potiphar and God. It took a real man to do that."

"And it took a real man to stand up to Big Bluffo today," said Mommi. "A sissy won't say no. But a real man or woman says no rather than hurt a friend."

Maxi didn't look sad now. He had a big smile on his face.

"Stand up Maxi," said Poppi. "We'd each like to come and shake hands with a strong man like Joseph."

Maxi's cheeks got a little red when his family shook hands with him. But it was fun. Now he was glad he had said no.

Growing Is . . . Being Faithful

What the Bible Story Teaches
God expects us to be faithful to Him and to those we love.

Thinking about the Bible Story
1. What did Potiphar's wife want Joseph to do?
2. How did Joseph show that he was faithful to Potiphar?
3. How do you know Joseph was faithful to God?

What the Muffin Story Teaches
It is better to be faithful, even if we get hurt for a little while. Things will work out right later.

Thinking about the Muffin Story
1. Why did Big Bluffo call Maxi a sissy? Was he? Why not?
2. Why did Poppi call Maxi a strong man? Was he? Why?

How Strong and How Weak?

How is each boy strong and how is he weak?

1. Pookie can run faster than Maxi, but he stole candy from him.
2. Charlie can throw a ball farther than Pookie, but he lied to him.
3. Big Bluffo can lift more than Charlie, but he looked at dirty pictures with the gang and Charlie said no.

The Bible Says
God will bless a faithful person (from Proverbs 28:20).

Prayer
Dear Jesus, You never did anything to hurt me. Teach me never to do anything that will hurt You or my family. Amen.

Don't Listen to Them!

Matthew 27:15,16; Mark 15:6-15; Luke 23:13-25; John 18:39—19:16

Pilate was worried. What should he do with Jesus?

Jesus' enemies had brought Him to Pilate. They wanted Pilate to put Jesus to death.

Pilate should have said no. He knew that Jesus had not done anything wrong. Why should he make Jesus die? That would please Jesus' enemies. But it would not be right.

Pilate did not say no. He tried something instead. "There is a rule that says I can free one prisoner," Pilate told Jesus' enemies. "Should I let Jesus or Barabbas go?"

Barabbas was a very bad man. Everyone knew that he should not get out of jail.

But Jesus' enemies began to stir up the people around them. "We want Barabbas, we want Barabbas," they said.

"What should I do with Jesus?" Pilate asked.

"Crucify Him, crucify Him," the crowd said.

Pilate should have said no. But he didn't. He would try something else. He would make the people feel sorry for Jesus. So he sent Jesus away. He had Jesus beaten with a whip. It had metal pieces at the end. Then soldiers pushed a crown of thorns over Jesus' head.

Pilate brought Jesus out for the people to see. Surely they would feel sorry for Him now. But they didn't.

"Crucify Him, crucify Him," they kept shouting.

Pilate should have said no. But he didn't. He gave up. He would do what the people wanted. He would send Jesus to be crucified. But first he had some people bring a bowl of water. Then he washed his hands in the water.

"You made me do this," Pilate said. "It's not my fault."

The people really didn't make Pilate do it. He could have said no. But he didn't.

Pilate let Barabbas go. Then he sent Jesus to be crucified. Pilate should not have listened to the people. But he did. He should have said no. But he didn't.

Just Say No!
A Muffin Make-believe Story Poppi told Maxi about His Toys in Toyland

Have you ever been to Toyland? Maxi and Mini have. It's a pretend place, you know. So it's all right to go there and do fun things with Maxi's toys.

Whenever Maxi and Mini pretend to go to Toyland they meet Maxi's toys. Whenever they pretend to go to Thimblelane Trails they meet Mini's stuffed animals. Today they are going to Toyland. It is a fun place to go.

Maxi and Mini marched with the wooden soldiers, jumped with Jack-in-the-Box, and spun with the beautiful tops. They even played games with Nutcracker and Windup Mouse.

But at last it was time to go home.

"We'll take you there," said the wooden soldiers. "We'll have a parade and march you right back home."

"That's not the way to do it," Mini whispered to Maxi. "Poppi said we should just pretend and we'll be home."

But the wooden soldiers already had their parade started. One tooted on the horn. Another clashed on the cymbals. Maxi and Mini didn't want to make the wooden soldiers feel sad. So they went with them.

The wooden soldiers marched around

and around. They kept on marching until Maxi and Mini were tired. But they never got Maxi and Mini home.

"We'll get you home," said the tops. "Come here and spin with us. Whirl around and around and soon you will be home."

"That's not the way to do it," Maxi whispered to Mini. "Poppi said we should just pretend and we'll be home."

But the tops were already spinning. Maxi and Mini didn't want to make the tops feel sad. So they spun around and around until they were dizzy. But they never got home.

"I'll get you home," said Jack-in-the-Box. "Come here and jump up and down with me. When you jump high enough, you can jump all the way home."

"No!" Mini and Maxi both said. "We know how to get home and that's what we're going to do right now!" So they pretended they were home. And do you know what? They were!

Growing Is . . . Listening

What the Bible Story Teaches
Don't listen to the wrong people. They will get you into trouble.

Thinking about the Bible Story
1. What did the crowd want Pilate to do? Did he HAVE to do it?
2. What would you like to say to Pilate?

What the Muffin Story Teaches
Listen to what you know is right.

Thinking about the Muffin Story
1. How did the wooden soldiers try to get Maxi and Mini home? Why couldn't they do it?
2. How did the tops try? Why couldn't they do it?
3. Who told Maxi and Mini how to get home? Why should they listen to Poppi?

Should You Listen to These?

Should you listen if:

1. Mommi says, "Stay away from that place"?
2. Poppi says, "Don't touch that"?
3. A friend says, "Let's do it! Your mother and father will never know"?
4. Jesus says, "Love Me"?

The Bible Says
Listen to Me, God says, and I will teach you what you should do (from Psalm 34:11).

Prayer
Dear Jesus, I trust You so I want to listen to You. Teach me to listen to others I trust too. Amen.

A MUFFIN APPLICATION • 77

PRAISING GOD BY SINGING

Singing to a King
1 Samuel 16:14-23

Saul could have been a good king. God wanted to help him. But Saul would not let Him. He wanted to do things his own way.

At last God went away from Saul. He let Saul do things his own way. Then an evil spirit came to be with Saul. He made Saul do things he really did not want to do. He made Saul sad.

Before long Saul began to yell at his servants. He said terrible things to his family and friends. Saul's servants knew they must do something. But what? Then one day a servant had a good idea.

"King Saul likes music," the servant said. "We must find someone who plays the harp. He will play and sing for the king. Then the king will feel better. He will treat us all better."

It really was a good idea. But who should they get. Then someone remembered David.

"He is brave and handsome and strong," the servant said. "And he plays the harp and sings well."

"Good!" said the other servants. Before long someone went to find David.

David was happy to go with the servant. He had played and sang many times for his sheep. This would be much better to play and sing for the king.

King Saul was happy to hear David's beautiful music. The sweet notes and words of David's psalms made him feel better.

The king was so pleased that he gave David a special job in the palace. For a long time David stayed in the palace and played sweet music for the king.

David liked to play and sing for his king. He was glad that he could make the king feel better. But he was even more glad that he could please God with his music.

Playing for Someone Special

"Have you practiced today Maxi?"
"No Mommi."
"When do you plan to do it Maxi?"
"Later Mommi."

That's the way it was. Maxi liked his guitar. But he didn't like to practice. But lots of boys and girls are like that, aren't they?

Maxi was still thinking about "later" when Poppi came home. "Do you know who's on TV tonight?" Poppi asked.

"Yeah, Gordon Hotfoot," said Maxi. "Someday I'm going to play just like him."

"Well, he's going to tell you how to do it tonight," said Poppi.

Maxi could hardly wait to turn on the TV that night. "Listen to him play!" said Maxi. "I'm going to play just like him."

At last Gordon stopped playing. "Some of you out there are just learning to play," he said. "I want to tell you two secrets."

"Here it is!" said Maxi. "That's for me!"

"First, practice every day," said Gordon. Maxi gulped. He tried not to look at Mommi.

"Second," said Gordon. "Think of someone special and play for that person."

After the program Maxi ran to get his guitar. "I'm going to practice every day," he said. "And I'm going to play for someone very special."

"Who's that?" asked Mommi.

"Jesus!" said Maxi. "If I play for Him, I will always do my very, very best."

A MUFFIN FAMILY STORY • 85

Growing Is . . .
Singing and Playing

What the Bible Story Teaches
We should sing and play to please God and others.

Thinking about the Bible Story
1. Why did King Saul need good music?
2. Why was David chosen to sing and play for Saul?
3. Who else was David trying to please? Do you think he pleased God? Why?

What the Muffin Story Teaches
Singing or playing for someone we love helps us give better music.

Thinking about the Muffin Story
1. What two things did Maxi learn about playing good music?
2. Why do you think these same two things helped David sing and play well?

When Should You Praise God by Singing?

Should you praise God by singing or playing music when:

1. You get something for which you prayed?
2. You know that Mother and Father love each other?
3. You talk to Jesus?
4. You want others to know how much you love Jesus?

The Bible Says

Sing and make music in your hearts to the Lord. Always give thanks to God the Father for everything (Ephesians 5:19,20).

Prayer

Dear Jesus, thank You for music. It's another way to say I love You. Amen.

A MUFFIN APPLICATION • 87

Praising God and Pleasing God
Nehemiah 8

"The walls are done!" the people shouted one day. All over Jerusalem people were excited. They were happy they had fixed the walls around Jerusalem.

The people had worked hard to fix these walls. When they started they had nothing but piles of stones. Long ago some enemies had broken down Jerusalem's walls. As the years went by dirt covered some of the stones. Those piles of stones and dirt were quite a mess.

But Nehemiah and his friends knew that God wanted them to build these walls again. They asked God to help them and He did. That's why the people worked together until the walls were done.

Now Nehemiah planned a time to praise and thank God at one of the gates. The people came from all over the land. They wanted to show God how happy they were that the walls were fixed.

The people became quiet as Ezra the priest stood on a wooden platform. They listened carefully as he began to read the Word of God from a scroll.

While Ezra read, some helpers walked among the people. They told the people what Ezra was reading and what it meant to them.

Ezra read a little from God's Word. Then he stopped to pray and praise God. The people said "Amen," and bowed their faces to the ground. That was their way to tell God how great He was and how they wanted to please Him.

Then Ezra read some more from God's Word. Again the leaders told the people what Ezra was reading and what it meant to them. That went on for hours.

Little by little the people began to understand what God's Word was saying to them. Little by little they began to understand that they had not been pleasing Him. That made them sad.

Suddenly someone began to cry. Then another person cried, and another. Before

long all the people were crying. That's because they were so sad that they were not pleasing God. Ezra and Nehemiah were sad too.

"Now it's time to stop crying," Ezra and Nehemiah told the people. "It is time to praise God that the walls are done."

So the people stopped crying. They began to praise God for all He had done. They kept on praising God for seven days. Don't you think they must have sung many psalms?

It's hard not to praise God when He does so much for us, isn't it? And it's hard not to be happy when you are praising God.

Sun Smiles and Cloud Tears

A Muffin Make-believe Story that Mommi Told Mini and Maxi

Everyone in the kingdom loved Prince Maxi. That's because he was like the smiling sun. Some said the sun smiled in the land because Prince Maxi smiled. So the land was always bright and beautiful. There were never dark clouds with tears.

"The smiling sun warms our kingdom and makes it beautiful," said some.

"And the dew waters the flowers and trees," said others. "We do not need dark clouds with tears."

As long as Prince Maxi pleased the king, the sun kept smiling. Some said the dark clouds with tears would come if he did not do this.

One day Prince Maxi got up on the wrong side of his bed. He looked in his mirror. He grumbled and complained. He thought he was bigger and better than he really was. He even thought he was bigger and better than the king.

"I do not want to please the king today," he said. So that's what he told the king. He even told Princess Mini. Then he told the people.

Just as some people expected, dark clouds with tears came over the land. The sun stopped smiling. Tears began to fall. They were cold, sad tears.

The king was sad. Princess Mini was sad. So were all the people. Even Prince Maxi was sad.

"This is no good," said Prince Maxi. "I will please the king again."

When he did, the dark clouds with tears ran away to hide. The sun began to smile again. Now the king was happy. Princess Mini was happy. And all the people were happy too.

But the next morning Prince Maxi got up on the wrong side of his bed again. He grumbled at the mirror. He began to think he was bigger and better than he was. He even began to think he was bigger and better than the king.

"I do not want to please the king today," Prince Maxi said. So that is what he told the king. He told Princess Mini. And he even told all the people.

Dark clouds with tears came again. The sun stopped smiling. Cold tears began to fall.

This made the king sad. Princess Mini was sad. And all the people were sad too.

"This is no good," said Prince Maxi. "I must please the king."

When he did the sun smiled again. The king was happy. Princess Mini was happy. And all the people were happy once more.

The next morning Prince Maxi got up on the wrong side of his bed again. He grumbled at his mirror. He almost thought he was bigger and better than he was. He almost thought he was bigger and better than the king. And he almost told the king, and Princess Mini, and the people that he would not please the king today.

But he didn't.

That's because he saw the king behind him. The king really was much bigger than Prince Maxi. Suddenly Prince Maxi knew that the king was stronger and smarter too.

Through one window Prince Maxi saw the bright sun waiting to smile on the kingdom. Through another window Prince Maxi saw the dark clouds, waiting to bring their cold, sad tears.

"I WILL PLEASE THE KING TODAY," Prince Maxi almost shouted. "I WILL SAY THINGS THAT PLEASE HIM, I WILL DO THINGS THAT PLEASE HIM."

Prince Maxi said that so loud that the dark clouds ran away to hide. The sun smiled on the kingdom.

The king was happy. Princess Mini was happy. All the people sang a happy song. So Prince Maxi was happy too. That's the way it is when we try to please God. He is the King we want to please each day.

A MUFFIN FAMILY STORY • 93

Growing Is . . . Pleasing God

What the Bible Story Teaches
Pleasing God will make you happy. If you don't please Him, it will make you sad.

Thinking about the Bible Story
1. What special work had the people finished? Did that make them sad or happy? Why?
2. What made the people cry? What helped them praise God again?

What the Muffin Story Teaches
We bring the most sunshine, joy, and happy songs to others when we please them and God.

Thinking about the Muffin Story
1. What caused the dark rainy cloud to come? What caused the sun to shine?
2. Why did Prince Maxi decide at last to please the king?
3. How does this remind you to please God?

How to Make the Sun Smile

Which of these will please God, and bring sun smiles? Which of these will not please God, and bring cloud tears?

1. Helping Mother with chores.
2. Thanking Father for fixing my bike.
3. Playing with brother or sister without arguing.
4. Telling Father I won't go to church.
5. Saying God's name in a bad way.

The Bible Says
Sing joyfully to the Lord (from Psalm 33:1).

Prayer
Dear Jesus, a smiling sun is so much better than cloud tears. You will help me bring smiling suns to my family and friends, won't You. Amen.